1   **THE POWER OF COMPASSION**

2   **THE LINK OF COMPASSION**

3   **LOVE AND COMPASSION**

4   **DEPROGRAM AND COMPASSION**

5   **TIMELESS COMPASSION**

6   **TRINARY AND COMPASSION**

7   **THIRD POINT AND COMPASSION**

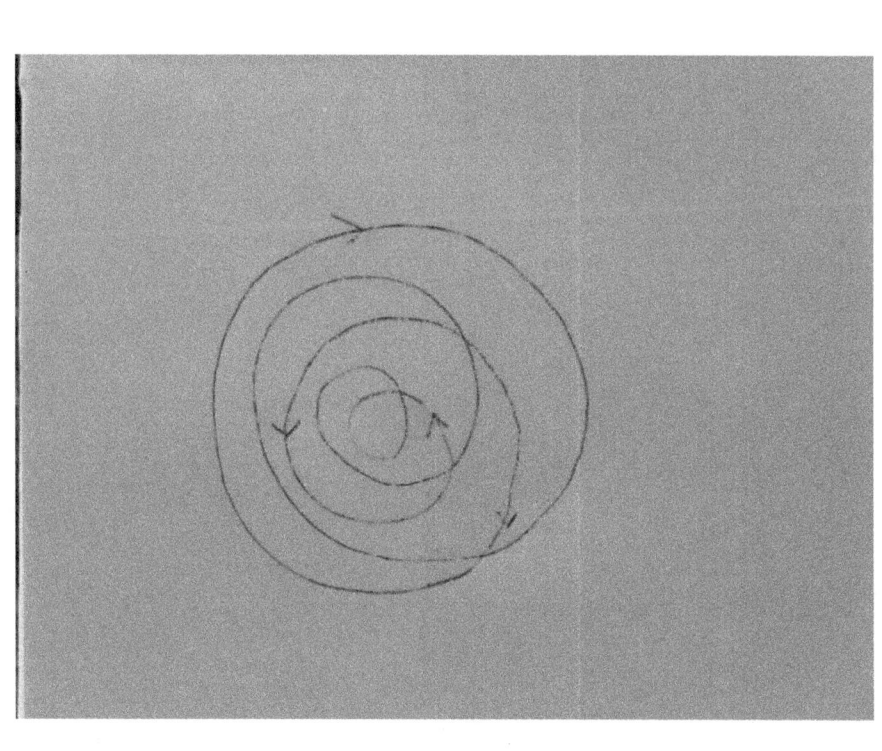

THE POWER OF COMPARISON

THERE ARE TWO SIDES AND THE MIDDLE
IN SHORT - TWO SIDES AND THE KEYS

IF THE THIRD BECOMES TWER
THEN THE MIDDLE WILL BE LOST

CHECK / BALANCE REQUIRES THREE SIDES
HOW TO STRENGTHEN THE MIDDLE FORCE?

THE LINK OF COMPASSION

BY THAT WE SEE THE GOOD IN THE BAD
THE GOOD/BAD IS STILL GOOD/BAD
BUT A LINK HAS BEEN ESTABLISHED

SOMETIMES LINKS FRIENDS
EVEN WHEN THEY ARE
FAR APART

WHEN LOVERS REUNITE
EVEN IF THEY MERGE INTO ONE
THERE IS STILL THE OTHER

LOVE AND COMPASSION

LET GO MALE / RECEIVE FEMALE

RECEIVE FEMALE / SHARE MALE

SHARE MALE / LET GO FEMALE

LET GO FEMALE / RECEIVE MALE

RECEIVE MALE / SHARE FEMALE

SHARE FEMALE / LET GO MALE

DEPROGRAM AND COMPASSION

DEPROGRAM THE OPPOSITE

WE ALSO CHANGE

DEPROGRAM THE FEMALE

THE MALE ALSO DEPROGRAMS

DEPROGRAM THE WEAKNESS

THE WEAKNESS STRENGTHENS

TIMELESS COMPASSION

IF LOVE IS THE URGE TO UNITE

COMPASSION THE URGE TO LIBERATE

LIBERATE THE URGE

LOVE/COMPASSION STILL THERE

TRIMARY AND COMPARISON

THREE DIFFERENT CLOCKS
24-HR : AM/PM : AM/PM OR THREE AM CIRCLES

THREE DIFFERENT CALENDARS
FORWARD, REVERSE AND/OR THREE CIRCLES

TRIMARY MORE THAN BINARY
YET THEY ARE THE SAME

THIRD POINT AND COMPASSION

"THERE IS INNER OUTER AND SECRET
DIMENSION"

IF INSIDE MERRY GO AROUND
THERE IS ONLY TWO DIRECTIONS ;
IF OUTER/INNER WORLDS MERGE
THERE STILL TWO DHAMMAS

THERE IS ALWAYS THREE SIDES
EVEN IF WE SEE ONLY TWO ;
THERE IS ONLY ONE WORLD
EVEN IF WE HAVE TO
SEE IT AS TWO

www.ingramcontent.com/pod-product-compliance
Lightning Source LLC
Chambersburg PA
CBHW061318040426
42444CB00010B/2692